_GHT

R ICHARD M ILES

ONION
RIVER

PRESS

Burlington, Vermont

Onion River Press
24 Maple Street, Suite 214
Burlington, VT 05401
www.onionriverpress.com

ISBN: 978-1-957184-39-5

Library of Congress Control Number: 2023913755

For Susan

Contents

Part Three

Part Four

Part One

Miracles

We lift our legs
so she can sweep
and as she does she says

My broom is a grass fire
set by ancient hunters
to grow new grass and bring the eland

and this was long before
they learned to cook with fire

so see how the miracle is
your feet to the flame
where soon it will be green

and not just here in the kitchen
but blinking in last night's sky
sacred the whole time

thanks for lifting your feet

Alight

Outside around sunset
a small dark bird (siskin?) floated
downward in soft waves like a feather
and gave me "alight"

her cursive flight and gentle landing
atop our apple tree
so considerate and timely
stirs the cells of the tree

Area Code

505 ABQ calls
867 Yellowknife
and a grizzly bear

picks up – So treasure
the silent forms in nature;
syllabic measure

for one, she tells me,
and the repetitions
we may sometimes see

in all the spirals,
tessellations, cracks and stripes,
fractals, symmetricals,

dunes and rings, meanders,
speeches, spots and stains, foam
and the gyri and sulci

of the human brain,
neurons firing as we search
our dark memories,

the calm spray
of galaxies, patterns of
rootlessness in a swamp,

price jumps in the market,
turbulence
under the flooded Nile—

all silent forms in nature,
and what about the
recent quincunx

of abstract painting
in Pollock's hand with
particle physics?

And picture the floating
silences Basho produced
from his lonely steps:

"Tremble, oh my grave –
In time my cries will be
only this autumn wind."

My Sundial

Time's compass runs
a little fast
slows for the moment
pressed into my gut
as though struck by
that *first glance*
of capture and release

an eclipse in the eye
with feathering corona
to offer and brush out
what comes next

Looking down the darkness

of the hand-dug well
the usual heap of echoes
and brain stones
darkness become sticky

at the bottom of the gaze
a knowing eye glints
tells you about funny
what it is and why it is
some funny fades   other funny stays

¾ Day Moon

Welkin's keyhole
missing puzzle piece
always there

afterthought of former moon
and her premonition

bird on a wire
before the wire

battered puck
soft elbow patch

perfumed neck rising
from a pearl

Surviving the Storm

birds' nests everywhere
daring nurseries
held like whole notes aloft
in stripped trees

sweet fearless voice
we thought we heard in the leaves
all summer and plaited
in the wind

Watermark

Let's see... the waters are clearing.
Looking around in the dark for I'm not sure what,
I bumped into you and you are still here.

Wait, don't go.
See the murky watermark down there
once so firmly pressed upon us,

does it resolve before our gaze
or dissolve?

This morning

from our kitchen window
two brown-flecked sparrows

intent on counterpoint
peck at pinheads in the tire tracks

sand to be teeth
for food grinded
in their gizzards

their stark activity unfolds as being
within the day

in their cheer
they enjoy the empty coherence
of everything they do

and for just such a *chip-chip*
they pause to make whole
an entire caress

Mother and I whispered

under beating stars
their frozen light

here just in time
to ask why we whisper

in just arrived light of stars long dead
I hear in her shielding breath

the alert silver interval
between chimes of star bells

prescient witness
to our binding fate

Indian Summer in My Indian Summer

A mix of twisted leaves
baking and mulching
in the woods at the feet of their parents

plump golden sun backs away
to linger at the door
keeping an eye on us
you're next it exhales
kneel here I wish to meet
your host to spread webbed light
my net over you

to tow you behind me
down tunneled slopes

She tells a story

her voice a descending trail with captive shadows
where one could pause for an overview
or slip between and enter her mind
of reflections and dreams braided
into this valley-ward trail
that from a distance might appear
as a ribbon binding the mountain

but if one stays on her voice's path
its sinuosities and breaths
form bridges where gaps have opened
between three distinct realms
the path the gorge the sky
and a Minerva ray escapes
in her eye

An Address

Here we are with our names
chosen by our parents
though most of us
by now adult orphans
identities fading
even our signatures
So pay your bills electronically
and like tonight's full moon
burst into nameless blossom
and scatter your petals on water

Evolove

How nearly evolve
contains love
backwards and forwards

fitting they're entwined
two states at once
in the bed of change

like a spider's thread
liquid inside
solid when exposed to air
and she exults in her web

Open up a place in its moment

flatten it out
expose a crevice
recess and desolation
scars and dark renewal

feel the breath
withheld in its history
lingering gestures
of being loved and played on

its voice and echo alternating
with a wash of sounds
a million intersections
chorus of one

imagine living somewhere
alert to the openings
when *in a certain slant of light*
normal eyesight drops away

and the sacred squeezes through

Ourselves the sky

as nowhere becomes now here
reflected in the pond

last night the many lifetimes
of clouds passing before the moon

made it full and fuller still
until it closed its eye with a gong

and we wrapped the field around us
sleeping like fallen fruit
in which the earth has risen

Part Two

Stepping

my right leg
into pants this morning
I think of Grandad

his farm on Twin Lakes
as a boy he walked four miles
to school   and his cave

What is there

to look for in this moment
nothing   it is dark outside
is it dark inside
it is a bright darkness brightened
by light on the other side

November 16th

kneels
sips from her own pond and reflects
reflects and sips

breezy her language evolves
in a passage between two sheets
dancing on the line

when dry and folded
their exchange hovers in the air
to query the last of day

November 25th

Thanksgiving, sunny

Ahead of me my shadow on the grass
greets my step
with my stride and arm swing
where was I going
and where am I from truly

at a certain point we turn
and back to back become
the shadow who never strode away

now I feel it pause within me
stirring gently like the sea
we walked beside

December 6th

By absorbing it
a patient day informs us
of steps to take or not to take
of some truths in the past denied
of what to eat
and how to prepare for the occasion
forming in the nearly visible future
out over a rain-hatched bay

December 10th

The chill inside a silver pitcher
a blur of snow

white toupees atop the stonewall
air thickened   a new element to trudge through

as if I've taken no step
I take the next one

when I turn for home
no tracks

December 21st *winter solstice*

Exhilarated by crisp December air
after a few sips the earth
tilts a bit on a hemisphere
and we have a pivot
in our fates

One senses a collision course
as in the east
the sun thrusts a flaming head from its covers
Tomorrow will be one second longer than today
and blanches at the day moon setting in the west

Somewhere on this stream

I fished around a corner of my life
and caught a trout

after releasing her I was never the same
we changed places

in her unknown waters
an immersion

nourished and aware
I followed the current

like the fish I put back
who slipped away

to return a bit
of what I was given

Heaven

Plumie, aged five, enters the kitchen with a crayon drawing.
She waves me over. Come here under the light, Daddy.
Here is our house and the barn and Nuggy and Lois and Fanny.
That is Mama cooking pancakes and you reading in your chair
with Nuggy.
This is you again milking Lois in the barn and I made one two
three four cows.
More is better. And this is their watering trough.
The wavy line is our stream with frogs and watercress.
It goes to the fat line—White Creek with trout. Spose to be trout.
I left out our road and car—too noisy.
Here's Mama in the garden with Nugget watching.
Those are our two hills with the moon going up while the sun
goes down way over here.
Remember? It is spring so I put buds on the trees and this is a
crocus flower.
You wouldn't know it if I didn't tell you,
and all this, Daddy, is the sky with muscle clouds.
See, here is Orion and the North Star and the Milky Way,
and these stars are spose to be Scorpio, your birthday.
It's the whole world. I made it!

Something follows me

of light or shadow
eyelash or breath

ear of the day
that slides its octave up and down

or dependent child
there because I am

here too it is
small cloud on the ground
I might step in and fall through

and when we reach a long rise
it clambers into me and hides

A Well

Dowsing
a well
or I am the water

Her Eyes

A landscape
of what they've seen
and washed into light
absorbing blue
shine of the visible
with suspended ghosts

Hurricane Carol, September 1, 1954

For a chance to match storms
climb the trusted
backyard maple tree
and wedge into the crow's nest

Listen at height
to wails of women
and hug the trunk
through keeling wind-blasts

Cold knots of rain
soak and lash

Hungry and shaking
pass through fear
nearly let go and fly

With the fear still clinging
like the walls of a tunnel

And afterward people
can see the tunnel

You give a word

your voice has carved
with all your life
that comes into being
when you say it

deep from your past
full and shining
cut with your accent
grown in the silence around it

Pruning the Grapes

A tribe of robins on the lawn
listens for the worm
as to the ganglia
trellised in my head

where to prune
the forbidding snarl

of lines worms and vines
no problem for the birds

loppers hover at a joint
the robins wait

Old Farmhouse with Canted Barn

I walked five miles up the wooded valley
along the descending Green River
until the land opened into meadows and I could see
an old farmhouse tucked in its cirque

as if a recollection awaiting my step
the reverse of a view I might always remember
but a sign of my life
where now I would dwell

as I felt on first seeing you
when our trails on the mountain crossed
and I knew we resumed
each other's lives

two strangers in the past together
walking with one foot after the other
to become who we had been
in the old farmhouse with its canted barn

At dusk

before the dark glass slider
a father's silhouette talks to me
or perhaps to his own future
with assurance impossible
in light of the steady demise advancing
through the drain of day
and deepening greens

He outlines the major points of manhood
a man's duty and what betrayals to expect
as if the game were over and won
it was not easy but he prevailed
secretly he wishes it had been more of a trial

His talk ends as his shape is swallowed by darkness
the day behind him has fully departed
without a trace of struggle
it resonates now
in the throat of night

Waves

The day your life ended ends
taking forever
everyone stands around

without you
to view it the world
is an awkward adolescent

a feminine shower
condensation of your spirit
absorbs the last blush in the sky

like the welcoming doors of your eyes
which people can see in the distance
as the you-raindrops

nicking each wave on the bay
to land on the earth where you knelt in your garden
where autumn and spring will meet

to exchange kisses tasting
of the three kinds of heart-wood
going into your coffin

Seeds of Elsewhere

How the hand holds a chisel
whether like a pencil for drafting
or a stirring stick or conductor's baton

how the other hand grips the hammer
and the rising arm takes aim
to describe the arc of its plunge

how the hammer strikes to shape the yearning stone
or to knock wedges set between feathers
in ⅜th-inch holes drilled along a score

the work reveals the person
a glimpse of inner contours
where granite fizzes before it splits

its grain straining to adhere
and the stone begins to part from itself
to reveal another order

reflexive logic gasps
as if riding a space probe
into fresh views of galactic structure

the locked door of the mind cracks open
strains and seeds of elsewhere waft in

The breeze at dawn

unfurls shadows of wood smoke
over the snowfield

where they gather
to form a trotting fox

she pokes her face in the snow
and snags a burrowed mouse

across my mind thoughts drift like smoke

the one that halts
for a moment and a picture

is the change in my handwriting
in seventh grade

a sudden shift
to another course

Part Three

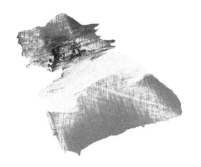

After or Before

She either stops writing
or the writing on the page ceases

she's gone beyond depletion
into emptiness
does she still have
a body   a face

she turns to
the mirror behind her
where there is no one
a void in the glass

she touches her unreflected eyes
tosses her hair and her laugh
shows as a watery ripple
through the air

she takes up her writing and begins
to read to the mirror

the moving mouth comes into view
nose and philtrum form
her least favorite features
forehead eyes and ovenbird hair

until fully armed
she stands before herself a stranger

Nameless

At a lunch counter
studying a board of sandwich options
in a town I rarely pass through
a voice behind me repeats
a sound over and over
that I come to realize is my name
and I turn around
to see if it is I

Atlantic Crossing, *The Empress of Canada*, 1969

Midnight   mid-May   mid-Atlantic
the lounge closes
on the afterdeck before an operatic wind
abandoned full moon
serape of cloud blown over her belly
fragmented icebergs skulk in this galaxy
cauldron of seasons
purple engine moan ongoing

the *Empress's* stacked shadow
ponders alongside on the water   we're ghosting

and over there
my shadow in the stern
about to jump into my dead brother's face
blossoming in the wake

I remove my clothes: necktie
shoes suit shirt underwear
and let them balloon out
into darkness

I watch them float away
much as they entered: unpiloted
disfigured   scared silly

and naked go down to my berth

A pen

lifted from my desk drawer
after ten years forgotten in the dark
does not trust me
nor the light washing over it

the darkness was rabid
the unspeakable got in
the light will turn on me
like closing a drawer

where I work as though dead
addressing the dark

Too late

to head back now
darkness descending under full sail
storm-soaked black clouds
mopping up what's left of the twilight
that held me here

now I'm stuck until tomorrow
in the spell of this spot
the notion of "tomorrow" empties
along the generous poise of the landscape

I too slip away
without a decision
to get home before dark

perhaps I'll die here if I haven't already
or "anyone who thinks they are going to die
has already died and doesn't know it"

(while I can I would like to propose
that this place is writing me over
in its own syntax and grammar)

In my dream

we ate the rainbow
choosing a color a day
from an array of fruit

held up over the lawn
and you who died sixty years ago
skiing into an icy tree

approached with a smile
and sweeping your arm you said
my death was just a dream you know

now you've dreamt me alive
from this whole sky of colors

Pear Thief

A white feathery insect
with a fuzzy blue head
sketches a human form in the fog
its outline glides up the pear tree
plucks a fruit
examines and bites it
winks like an uncle

The muted autumn skies
call quietly for order
and a plangent wind obliges
chasing away the plundering fog

The Kiss

Her face with shadowy shoals in its depths
is the face of tossed ships and incipient storm
a face you suddenly see in a rock formation
set in a remote canyon

afraid of her   I kiss her
and the marble ledge we balance on
yields in its cells and we drop
into the bottomless blue

> "... It droppeth as the gentle rain from Heaven..."
> *William Shakespeare, The Merchant of Venice*

With the highest pine cone within my reach
a thin limb snaps
and from the top of the tall tree
I fall past my brother on a lower bough

forgotten instants flash by in stills
I see my life of ten years
in the five-second fall

not as memories deeply felt
but inevitable   unstrained as mercy

the drop from that shimmering pine
through an aerial tracery of gazes
(my brother's nearly catching me)
pierces the living world

I am rung like a bell
my body bouncing off branches as gravity itself
and the corpse on the ground who receives it

All-ee all-ee in-come-free

sings her boy cousin
but it is too late
other cousins found
relieved the game is over
she remains moment by moment
crouching through dusk
so hidden she is her own shadow
her own burrow
with only a burrow's dark eye
not even the animal
and seekless
taking hold in deep summer dirt
as the wind combs through stars

Rooming House

Around this dank bed in a rented room
a discrete weather of devious hours
streams before the mirror

furious to realize itself
each moment negates another
fermenting a silence loud in my sleep

dreams stick to the walls
like surgically removed adhesions
I shoulder them and climb

the summit is entry at daylight
with someone's life
dropped on my chest

and an appalled premonition
seeing itself
retreats to its fetid lair

Buck Hill Road

On our bulky 1950s bikes, my brother and I cross the tracks
and turn onto the dirt of Buck Hill Road. The first 100 yds. are
the steepest and no matter how hard we pump we have to get
off and push our bikes up to the corner by Alf Buck's house,
where the road levels and we can ride again. We never see Alf
Buck, but passing his house in the car at night what we take to
be his kitchen is dimly lit. Next driveway on the left is Burt and
Dottie Immin's house. One night after a few martinis at The
Arlington Inn Burt swallowed a fish bone and choked to death.
Once in a while Dottie would stop by on a charity drive to sit
with Dad and gossip. The next little house on the right, tucked
into the slope, has a sign on a tree painted in white letters: OLP.
Another invisible neighbor, but as we pass by one of us says,
"Olp! Excuse me!" We laugh and pedal faster, then sit back on
our seats, falling into private reveries and the sadness waiting in
our dark home and the deepening void of our mother's death.
Beyond our house, Buck Hill Road ends at the Congdons,
Wheaten and Helen, both in their 80s. Wheaten played the organ
on Sundays and occasionally fell asleep during Rev. Belcher's
sermon, collapsing on the keys and producing a long dissonant groan.

After the game

I feel as if the world were a friendly boy
walking along in the sun.
　　　　　　　–Robert Rauschenberg

Rules and maneuvers over
he climbs the hill to his home
loosely plucking spinning and slinging
the odd stone into the sun
dance that collapses in laughter
world and sun
going his wobbly zigzag way
hurler and hurled
giddy stone

the target un-aimed at
and hit

Rainbow Over the Organ Mountains Viewed from the Parking Lot of Sprouts Market, Las Cruces, New Mexico

Red orange yellow green blue violet
the flow of the spectrum
sweeps over a range of twisted spires
as they make themselves up
from eruptions of granite and rhyolite magma
an ephemeral crown bridging eons

The deluge in zinc sheets
hits the pavement
and fractures into grape-sized drops
to swamp the streets

Cars swoosh cars into transparence
a stoplight's hieroglyph eye
squints in spurts of traffic

The rain   its torrent become dripping ostinato   pauses

And having witnessed a terrible truth and survived
people emerge from Sprouts bearing bags of groceries
smiling madly

Bridges in their eyes

Tour

With no memory of how we got here
though following a guide,
almost as if the place were within us,
we came to a dirt clearing in the forest
about the size of a tennis court,
well-tamped and swept,
with two firepits of stone at either end,
neat stacks of dry split oak by each.

This open space was deeply still,
holding its breath,
neither a rustle of leaf nor nodding fern,
a moment suspended
in the center of movement.

The surrounding curtain of woods seemed not to be made of trees
but rather a dark and solid wall, though of a substance
one could walk into and perhaps through,
like the wall of a capsule containing a vivid dream
beyond which in the ether
lay the vaster space of things becoming.

A black wall between life and death
with rare porous points
where one bled into the other, the other into one.

And this area is where once a year
we gather to roast and consume our children,
our guide told us matter-of-factly.
Select children, of course, they're chosen at birth
and proudly grow to their sacrifice at the age of three or four,
drenched with damp herbs
and roasted slowly on a spit.
Empty your minds, pause and take a shallow breath.

Deer in Cold Rain

He'd had a good rainy Saturday in April. He'd finished a theme for class on Monday about how his stocking cap got caught in the rope-tow and almost dragged him headfirst into the pulleys before the engine tripped. He took a break to snitch a cookie. He felt in control and already approved of for doing his homework, especially on a spring Saturday when most school kids were stir-crazy. He usually disliked kids who were approved of and seemed in control, and he wondered who he really was. Out the window and under his nose four deer were calmly eating the early growth of his mother's daylilies. The easy way they munched in a soaking cold rain at dusk – paradise! Everyone knew that deer hair was hollow and insulated the animal from cold, but cold soaking rain?! Come on! Shivering for the deer, he grabbed a raincoat and went outside to be closer to them, to feel their magic. They looked up, wide-eyed, astonished. Was he real? How had he materialized? Their long eyelashes dripped rain and their neat hooves shone in the wet garden dirt. When they turned to run their tall white tails waved as if brushing paint on the dusk-silver canvas. He could just make out the painting and it was a faraway story in which none of them, not the deer, himself and his mother, their house, or the world they lived in, even figured.

I round a bend

a long straightaway opens up
with the sun standing at the end of the road
loyal old friend who knows I'm coming
or friend I'll meet in the future

I'm forgiven by both
they know by the time I reach them
I'll have walked my flesh away
and have only spirit to offer

Part Four

What I say

will be said back
by everything
by everything
I mean scintilla
that already know what
I might say

let's eat more light
like the giraffe
eating the light-eating
foliage that fears
the offhand lips
we say O.K.
to this morsel

On the mud flats

a black staple
digs clams

in the same spot
as yesterday

works upside-down
like a nuthatch

tide blushes green
envying itself again

gulls throw wide
a woven space

The Attic of an Oak

I spend all day standing in a bucket
high in trees
excising rot and dead limbs
cabling bifurcated trunks
shaping crowns for wires to pass through

we can keep a tree intact
or drop it and reduce it to chips

many trees have black spaces
high in their overstory
gaps where rogue forces congest
and hang as patient dark pockets
waiting to drop and attach to life below
like a tick or lamprey eel

sometimes caught in my work
I maneuver the bucket headfirst
into such a clot
eldritch and prickly
clinging to my face and hair
tangling my thought

other times cleaning the attic of an oak
from a dark area
a raven materializes
falls a bit before lifting away with angry flaps

around me the tree breathes
bends closer
deepens in color

Betweenities

(For Jesse, Easter, 2023)

Gaps between thoughts
between inhales and exhales
between striking the singing bowl
and the penetration of its chime
a moment not a person
but one with everything in the darkness

between heartbeats

Trudging through the woods
the bear vanishes as he stops
to rise on two legs
and scratch his back on a tree
that special tree
with its rough bark

For Years

piece by piece
I gathered tons of stone
for a long wall
to echo the range of mountains
far off in the west

and pulsing within it
the waves of our shore
beaten exchange
of water with stone

I thought of how mountains
condescend to the ocean
if they only knew

It grew dark
with sore hands I raised my maul
and split a block of granite
bright bone of the mountain
into a spray of stars

Once Wordsworth

The encircling mountains gain courage
move close
open their wide doors

It is hard at first to leave an open setting
animate inner country without boundary
in the wind off the Cumbrian Lakes

But inside the mountain
in the concinnity of soil once Wordsworth
medallion traceries of the mole

Veins of minerals and webs of water
architecture of worm and insect
are almost aflame

And then like limbs of oak
the bones "being stricken one against the other
break out likc fire & wax greene"

Fulgar Conditum

Fifteen feet away the wall phone
hangs motionless on its black coils
my body flung across the room
I come to in a corner
burnt alive
by lightning riven in my left ear

you vanished for five minutes
says my friend still on the line

drinking *fulgar* with the gods
who birthed and nearly slayed me
we got drunk and battled
some of me is buried

fused to the earth
charge still searing my brain
a divine connection strengthened
annealed and fertile
a pregnant man

Even now

as a well-trained human obedient
to maxims and mercilessly educated
I refer to a tabula rasa to make decisions

this blank slate is always there
though I be tarred in sin it shines unblemished
in a cave without walls
a glossy pool of souls

can there be anything mine
separate from this pool

in any case it calls the shots
and me in human form
pulls the trigger
let's see what happens

Walking Around the World

A life in every step
builds the world
like a hand for each stone
the temple

I strode through
was it fear   more a distance
into whorled air
some confuse with ending

when we came face to face
the earth softened
now I walk in place
turning the globe

Rabbits for free

the doves announce over and over all over town
except for the ones calling Chickens for Free
and a few others on the bass Six Two Two Six Two Two
it all sounds good to me where would I go?
I've already got a few chickens
but could I use a rabbit?
I'm always up for the Tickets for Free
they sometimes offer
my presence doesn't mute them
as it does peepers in spring
the doves are safe and well above me
they want me to hear them they want me to want
Rabbits Chickens and Tickets for Free
and to see where they are

A wind from the future

blows over me in my waking this morning
or it's what my years will tell
when I blow out of life one day

the wind has a stropped edge
as the moist caul on things dries
and they shine in the sunrise

in a cloak of breeze
I walk by a doorway
where people from the past
are waiting to pass through

The other night

chopping vegetables
I faded away
into my grandson
now five
as a father himself
in a beach house
preparing a chowder
with his two little girls belting out
"Way down yonder in the paw-paw patch!"

His wife is out on her bike
giddy with freedom and beauty
wrapped in the glistening
breeze of her ride
bike-lamp charger ticking in the spokes:
mortal / immortal

twelve ears of sweet corn
nested in her handlebar basket

The view

from the window
over the pond
to the sage eye of the bay
does not need me in order to stay
it stays here
as I helped make it
by my soaking gaze

and when it is
here without me
no hole will be there

Provender

I've been washed
wrapped in linen
locked in a wicker trunk
and dropped into the earth
under a wide-armed oak

early decay smells sweet
like fresh peaches
the interludes between rotting
a long train ride
where departure and destiny merge

when I begin
to dissolve with the linen and wicker
my oak feeds and neighbor trees reach
with tendril roots
until I am all gone

in sunken ground
a few teeth
and the brass lock last the longest

From the crow's nest

the bird and the earthworm
are one and the same being
the supreme proof of water is thirst
the rabbit and wolf
are the same being
the world is my hunger
bite into it and also be grass
breathe deeply the icy air
and swallow sunshine
silver vintage of a pyramid

Hoofprints

of deer in fallen
tamarack needles
nobody home

beautiful rust
this much sap
for stark majesty

Grasslands

At any speed the train
was going nowhere
but deeper into a nether world
without destination

at the next stop
an empty platform
decrepit luggage wagon
a doorless lobby
where echoes of previous travelers
hover around your own
echoes that broke you

from somewhere in the waiting room
a solitary cricket in perfect pitch calls out
pure aimless fertile song

its song abruptly ceases
evaporates in shadows
collapsing the room
leaving a breath of perfume

The man in the field

becomes two men
what are they doing

are they fighting
is there a sort of exchange

between them and the field
usually men in a field

move in a game
but now there is no ball

they just stand in the wind
become one man again

Splitting Light

Orchard's voice calls
after the threshing wind

time to cut kindling
they call it "splitting light"

take the small camp axe
no need for the maul

and steer the wheelbarrow
through downed limbs

to saw ten-inch lengths
from the thicker fruitwood

straight enough to set
and strike free-standing

the thin random slices
thumb-width to sliver

that fly off the log
as if they were feathers

the last of the heartwood
is almost transparent

eyes of the light
inside the tree

bright as the flames
of the fire next year

Notes

p. 18 In "Open up a place in its moment" the words in italics are the first line of Emily Dickinson's poem #320.

p. 49 In "Too late" the quotation is from José Saramago's *The Stone Raft*.

p. 70 In "Once Wordsworth" the quotation is from John Lyly's *Euphues*.

p. 71 "Fulgar Conditum" translates as "Here Lightning is Buried".

Richard Miles' poems have appeared in various publications and journals, including *The New Yorker* and *The Beloit Poetry Journal*. His previous books are *Boat of Two Shores* and *Child*. He is a retired stonemason and sculptor in stone. He lives with his family on the coast of Downeast Maine, near a lighthouse, The Nash Island Light, which he and his son and friends restored.

Milton Keynes UK
Ingram Content Group UK Ltd.
UKHW020159241123
433040UK00011B/173